D1433336

PET OWNER'S GUIDE TO
Puppy Care & Training

SECOND EDITION

John & Mary Holmes

RINGPRESS

Published by Ringpress Books,
a division of Interpet Publishing,
Vincent Lane, Dorking,
Surrey, RH4 3YX, UK.
Tel: 01306 873822 Fax: 01306 876712
email: sales@interpet.co.uk

SECOND EDITION First published 2003

ISBN 978 1 86054 298 5

Printed and bound in Hong Kong through Printworks International Ltd.

CONTENTS

1 TAKING ON A PUPPY

Taking on a puppy is a major commitment, and it is something that should never be rushed into.

With luck, you are looking forward to a relationship that will last 12 to 14 years, so your choice of dog should never be decided on a whim or on an impulse.

There is little doubt that the majority of dog problems arise because so many people buy the wrong puppy or dog. It is like marrying the wrong person – you either have to make the best of a bad job, or make a break and start again.

However, the difference with owning a dog is that you have taken on an animal that is totally dependent on you for all its needs. This relationship should never be abused. The responsible dog owner must appreciate that, if you take on a dog, it is for life.

The Responsibilities

The first responsibility is to the dog, who, in return for the love and devotion he so willingly gives, deserves to enjoy a

Choose the type of pup that will suit your lifestyle.

reasonable quality of life. In order to enjoy life to the full, your puppy needs mental, as well as physical, exercise. He needs to live like a dog, not like a human – rolling in the grass, and, in permitted areas, allowed to gallop freely without the restriction of a lead. Your second responsibility is to other members of the community. You must ensure that the dog is under control at all times, and you must be prepared to 'clean up' after him.

GETTING OFF TO THE RIGHT START

Despite all the best intentions, the relationship between dog and owner can go sadly wrong. In fact, most problems that dog owners have to cope with could, and should, be avoided by the use of a little common sense, and by starting off with the right puppy. Perhaps the most important point to remember is that more can be learned about a puppy from his ancestry than from the puppy himself.

This is why a purebred puppy is less of a 'pig in a poke' than a mongrel. At least you have some idea of what the purebred puppy will grow

Litter-mates may look similar, but there can be huge character differences.

up to look like, which is impossible with a mongrel.

Although a pedigree puppy is likely to grow up resembling his parents, not all the puppies in the litter will have the same characteristics – far from it. But it is this false assumption that is probably the commonest mistake made by would-be puppy buyers, and it leads to many square pegs that will not fit into round holes!

IMPORTANCE OF INHERITANCE

So, which should you have? There are some 400 breeds of dog worldwide, and breed books have been written about most of the better-known breeds, containing detailed descriptions.

The weakness of many breed books is that they are often written by enthusiasts who see their breed through rose-coloured spectacles. Moreover, the author is labelled a traitor by fellow breeders if there should be so much as a hint of weakness in the breed. As a result, the good points of the breed are very often stressed – or even exaggerated – and any bad points are ignored.

The Root of Fear

A puppy inherits his characteristics from both parents, but some of these are more inheritable than others. According to Dr Malcolm Willis, the well-known geneticist, the most inheritable characteristic is fear.

This is not surprising when we consider that the dog is descended from the wolf. The bold, fearless wolf would very soon be a dead wolf, while the shy, furtive wolf would live to pass its genes on to future generations.

A fearful or nervous dog is almost invariably an unhappy dog. It can also be, and often is, a dangerous one.

Nervousness is the cause of the vast majority of people, including children, being bitten by their own dogs.

Like mother like son – or daughter! It is essential to assess the dam when viewing a litter.

UNDER MUM'S INFLUENCE

For the first six weeks or so of his life, a puppy is entirely under the influence of his dam. The pup will watch his mother and will learn from the way she behaves. If she is outgoing and friendly, he will behave in the same way. If she is nervous and fearful, he will copy these reactions. Experiments have shown that nervous bitches produce nervous puppies, even when these have been fostered from another bitch. Never buy a puppy without seeing him with his mother. Initially, see how the bitch reacts when you approach her puppies. If she is wary or aggressive, you will know that her temperament is unsound, and she may pass this weakness on. If she is not the sort of dog you would like to own, do not buy the puppy. Take time to look at lots of litters. If you make the right choice, you will have many years of fun and companionship to look forward to. Make the wrong choice, and you will have years to regret it.

PREPARING FOR YOUR PUP

Once you have decided to take on a puppy, you will need to make quite a few preparations before your puppy arrives home. If possible, decide on the puppy's name in advance. Everything will be strange to him, and, if the family are trying out different names on him, he will only become confused. If you cannot come up with the right name, just call him 'Puppy' until you do. Nearly all pups are used to coming to the sound of "Puppy, puppy" when the breeder has been calling the litter, and so your puppy should respond to this.

Check the safety of your house and garden to ensure there are no hazards for an inquisitive puppy. Trailing electrical wires are magnets to pups, and they can cause fatal accidents. Flimsy coffee tables, standing lamps, and ornaments on low tables are all accidents waiting to happen.

Outdoors, make sure there are no slug pellets lying around. These are very attractive to dogs, but they are poisonous and can have disastrous consequences if eaten.

The garden should be thoroughly puppy-proofed before bringing home your new addition.

BUYING EQUIPMENT

Feeding Bowls

Your puppy will need two feeding bowls, one for food and one for water. Bowls made of stainless steel are recommended. Although they are more expensive than other types, they are virtually indestructible, and they are easy to keep clean.

Brush and Comb

Few small puppies need very much grooming. However, you should get your puppy used to a grooming routine before it becomes a necessity – particularly if you have a long-coated breed. At this stage, all you will need is a good-quality brush and comb. The puppy's breeder is the best person to advise you on this.

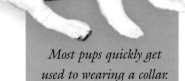

Most pups quickly get used to wearing a collar.

Collar and Lead

It is a good idea to get your puppy used to wearing a collar right from the start. Once he is used to wearing a collar, you can start lead-training. A light, buckled leather or soft nylon

A young puppy should get used to the routine of grooming from an early age.

collar is best, and you will need a fairly long, light but strong lead.

Identification

In the UK it is illegal for a dog to be in a public place without a collar and tag with a name and address on it. Many breeders now have their puppies tattooed before they are sold. Another form of identification is the micro-chip, which is painlessly implanted under the loose skin between the dog's shoulders.

EVERY PUPPY NEEDS TOYS

A puppy must chew – it is part of growing up. Pet shops are full of all sorts of canine toys and it is worth getting a few. Make sure they are good quality, as all too many pups have to undergo surgery to remove bits of rubber, etc. from their stomach after chewing unsuitable toys. The best sort to buy are those made from hard rubber; certain nylon chews are also good and safe. If you are buying a ball, make sure it is large enough so that it cannot be swallowed.

Beds and Bedding

A warm, draught-proof bed is essential. There are numerous types of dog bed on the market, but until the pup has stopped growing – and chewing – a plain cardboard box is perfectly adequate. Place the box on its side so that it makes a safe 'den' for the puppy.

Bedding needs to be warm and washable. We always use synthetic fleece fabric. This reflects body heat, it is non-allergenic and is difficult to chew. It is also free-draining, which means that you put newspaper under it and the upper side stays dry.

Dog Crates

Last, but not least, buy a folding dog crate. These are expensive but they last a lifetime, and the benefit both you and your dog will get from it should far outweigh the initial expense.

By nature, dogs like to have a 'den' that they can call their own. A crate makes a very satisfactory substitute. It is a great help with house-training, and it makes a safe refuge for the puppy when he wants to sleep, eat his dinner, escape from tiny, clutching fingers, rowdy teenagers, or even from you, his owner, if you are busy or in a bad mood!

A crate is invaluable when raising a puppy.

A dog who is used to a crate will learn to be relaxed when shut up in a confined space. So if your dog ever has to stay overnight at the vet, or goes to stay in boarding kennels, he will suffer far less stress if he is crate-trained.

Never use the crate for punishment. The whole idea is for the puppy to have a den of his own to enjoy. Do not shut him up for long periods during the day, but start with just a few minutes and gradually increase the time.

If you are busy around the house or going out for a short while, put the puppy in the crate for safety, but remember that the crate is a place of temporary refuge – it is not your puppy's home.

FINDING A VET

If you do not already know of a good vet in your area, you will need to find one before your puppy arrives home. If you have bought your puppy locally, the breeder will probably be able to help, or you can ask other dog-owning friends for a referral in your neigh-bourhood. Go along to see the vet before you bring the puppy home. Some puppies may have received their first inoculation, but you will need to find out what the inoculation programme is in your neighbourhood. Your puppy will almost certainly have started a worming programme, but you will need advice about further treatments over the next six months. A number of veterinary practices run 'puppy parties', which are great for socialising puppies, so you can ask about this at the same time.

COLLECTING YOUR PUPPY

Try to collect your puppy early in the day so that he will have time to settle in before evening. Take a friend or a member of the family along with you to help.

There are different opinions as to the best way to transport the pup. We would never put a puppy straight into a crate or a box in the back of the car. It seems cruel to take the pup away from his mother and siblings and then put him in a strange place and drive off. You want this puppy to like you and trust you – and this does not seem like a good start!

Friend's Lap

We suggest that you settle the puppy in your friend's lap, or, if he is a big puppy, let him lie next to your companion on the seat. Put a collar and lead on your puppy. In the excitement of arriving home, the pup could easily slip out of the car, which is the last thing you need.

Take along plenty of newspaper and old towels. Then, if the pup

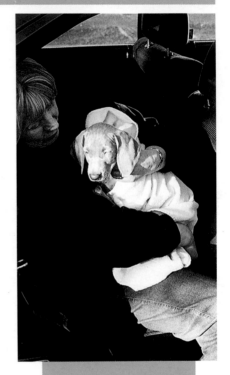

Arrange to travel with a 'helper' who can care for the pup on the journey home.

vomits – and he probably will – any mess can be mopped up without any trouble. Do not reprimand the puppy for being sick – it is not his fault.

PAPERWORK IS A MUST

Make sure you have all the necessary paperwork, such as vaccination certificates, record of worming, pedigree and transfer of ownership form (if applicable), and a certificate of tattooing or micro-chipping if this has been done. You will also need a diet sheet, and most breeders will willingly supply you with enough food for the first few days.

ARRIVING HOME

Take the pup out quietly and let him explore the garden. Do not ask all your neighbours and friends to come to admire him, and try to pick a time when the children are at school! Your puppy will have quite enough to get used to without being overwhelmed by lots of new people.

Once your puppy has relieved himself, he can be taken into the house, preferably confined to the kitchen or utility room. Offer the puppy a meal, play with him for a while, and, when he is relaxed and hopefully tired, let him sleep.

THE FIRST NIGHT: HOW TO HELP

You should have already decided where the puppy is to sleep, and this will probably be in the kitchen or utility room. If you are using a crate, make sure it is ready with a bed inside and the door open. Your puppy can have his first meal there, and you can encourage him to go in and have a nap during the day.

At night, take your puppy out to relieve himself just before you go to bed, and have a game with him in the hope of making him tired.

Then, put the pup to bed with a toy. He is bound to miss his siblings and the familiar surrounding. We have found that a well-wrapped hot-water bottle (not too hot) and an old alarm clock, which will help to break the silence, can both be useful. The puppy will almost certainly whine or yap, but, if you are lucky, he will soon settle down.

However, some pups can keep on whining for hours and hours. Remember, he is not doing it to

Some pups can be very persistent in their protests, but sleep will come at last.

YOUR NEW PUPPY TO SETTLE IN

annoy you – the poor puppy is homesick. But do not make the mistake of going to give him a cuddle. This will just make him shout louder in the hope that you will come back again.

If you really cannot stand the noise, take the puppy, in his crate, into your bedroom. Once he is used to the crate during the daytime, you can gradually get him used to staying in another room at night.

Do not take the puppy on to or into your bed. You could be storing up trouble in the future, especially if your baby pup is going to grow into a sizeable adult!

HOUSE-TRAINING

All young animals born in nests want to keep their living quarters clean. This is why it is easy to house-train a pig but almost impossible to house-train a chimpanzee! No one wants a dog to be dirty in the house, but, approached sensibly, house-training should be no big problem.

Do not start nagging at the puppy the minute you get him home, and do not make a drama out of it. Puppies who have been properly reared, with the opportunity to go outside to

Frequent trips outside are an important element of successful house-training.

19

relieve themselves, or those used to going on paper, are usually easy to teach.

First, decide on an area of the garden or yard you want your puppy to use. Then choose a word or phrase to encourage him to do what you want. We use "Hurry up"; some people use "Get busy". It does not matter what you say, as long as you always use the same words. Never put the puppy out alone. Always go with him and stay with him until he performs. Tell him to "Hurry up" in an encouraging tone, and, as soon as he does what you want, repeat the phrase and give him lots of praise.

Do not be in too much of a hurry to rush back inside. Many pups, and adult dogs, eliminate more than once, so give your

Let the new puppy explore the garden before taking him inside.

puppy a chance to empty his bowels completely. Then have a short game, and go back inside.

TELL-TALE SIGNS

Puppies usually give signs of wanting to relieve themselves. Some turn around and around, others sniff the ground, scratch, look round, whine, or suddenly squat down. An observant owner – and you will need to be one – soon learns what to look out for.

DON'T WORRY AT NIGHT

To start with, your puppy will be unable to last all through the night. Some conscientious owners get up during the night and take the puppy out, which undoubtedly speeds up house-training. But do not worry if you are not the sort who relishes waking up at 2am. Leave some newspaper on the floor, and, if your puppy dirties the paper during the night, just clean it up; he should eventually grow out of it.

MAKING MISTAKES

If your puppy makes a mistake in the house when you are not there, do not punish him, as he will have no idea what he has done wrong.

Occasionally, a puppy may not seem to have inherited the instinct to be clean, or the instinct has been weakened because the puppy has been forced to live under conditions where he had no alternative to being dirty.

With this type of pup, you will need to be even more vigilant. As soon as you see signs of him squatting, pick him up very quickly, telling him "No" in a harsh voice, and take him outside. Do not shout – it will not help. Stay with the puppy, even if it is a long wait. Tell him to "Hurry up", and, when he finally performs, make a really great fuss of him, telling him how clever he is.

Never get angry if your pup makes a mistake with his house-training.

21

2

FAMILY LIFE

In the first few weeks in his new home, your puppy will learn to interact with all members of the family. It is vitally important that you supervise all interactions in the early stages, so that relationships get off on the right footing.

GETTING ON WITH CHILDREN

Children and puppies should have a natural affinity with each other. It has been proved that children who play with animals early in life tend to be more open-minded, and make more effort to understand others, than children who have not had this opportunity. Puppies and children growing up together can form a lasting and rewarding relationship.

However, you must use common sense. No matter how accustomed to your dogs your children are, nor how good-tempered your puppy, never leave a small child or baby alone with a puppy. Disasters can – and do –

happen very quickly. A large pup can push a toddler over, and that child may be frightened of dogs for life. Sharp puppy teeth can easily puncture a baby's skin, unintentionally, but still painfully. Small hands clutching a tiny puppy can really hurt; and a child who does not know how to pick up a puppy properly may drop it.

If you do not have any children of your own, then beg, borrow or steal some! With all the anti-dog laws, now common in most places, it is vital that your puppy learns to associate with children. If your pup is reluctant to go to children, do not force him.

Take Your Time

Take time, use plenty of praise and treats, and make sure your puppy only meets children who are good with dogs until he is comfortable with them.

If you have children of your own, they must be taught to respect the pup and not to treat him as a toy to be picked up, carried about and then dropped on the floor. Make sure the children learn to leave the pup alone when he is in his crate or sleeping in his bed, and when he is eating.

Children should be encouraged to participate in the puppy's care and training.

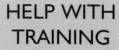

HELP WITH TRAINING

Most children over the age of seven or eight can help with training. When it is the pup's feed time, let the child call the pup and ask him to "Sit" (see Chapter Six); and then reward him with his food. Children can also practise the "Down" using a treat as a reward. But make sure this is not done too often; once or twice is enough. Older children should be able to take the puppy out on a lead although they should be accompanied by an adult.

FELINE RELATIONS

If you have a family cat who is used to dogs, as long as you do not let the puppy chase the cat, everything should be okay.

However, cats are unpredictable creatures and you cannot tell how a cat who is unaccustomed to dogs is going to react. Some will attack a small puppy, such as a

Yorkshire Terrier; others go beserk, climbing up the curtains and spitting furiously. Fortunately, most family cats are tolerant creatures – they have to be – and a little common sense should be all that is needed.

Your pup is almost certain to want to investigate this strange creature (unless he has been brought up with cats), so introduce them under controlled conditions in the house.

- Put the pup on a collar and lead, and, if the cat just sits and stares, or bristles slightly, let the pup approach gradually.
- If the cat decides to take off, stop the pup from chasing it and try again later. Never let the pup chase after the cat, yapping.
- Some cats will give a 'nosy' pup a hefty swipe with a paw. If the pup is large and bouncy, it will do him no harm and will probably make him more respectful next time.
- However, if you have a small puppy, try not to let this happen as it could scare him or even hurt him.

Cats and dogs usually learn to respect each other.

MAKING FRIENDS WITH SMALL PETS

If you have pet rabbits or guinea pigs, they will probably be in hutches, cages or outside runs, so they should be safe from small puppies – but do not let the pup run round and round yapping at them.

Introduce the puppy quietly, and check him with a harsh "No" if he refuses to leave them alone. Find something else for the puppy to do, play ball with him or give him a favourite toy. He should soon start accepting your small pets and lose interest, but never leave him alone with them.

THE RESIDENT DOG

Many people consider the idea of having a new puppy before the family dog becomes too old. In this way, the loss of the older dog is often eased. However, think carefully before going ahead with this plan.

Never bring in a young pup if you have a chronically sick, old dog, or one that suffers from arthritis or a similar joint illness. A stiff and creaky old granddad does not want small grandchildren crawling all over him – much as he may love them. The same goes for the old dog.

However, if you have an old dog who enjoys the company of other dogs, who has slowed down and mellowed, and perhaps lost some of his former drive, a puppy may give him a new lease of life.

In The Garden

When the puppy arrives home, introduce the pup and the old dog in the garden, where there is more space, and give them time to check each other over. You are, or should be, the pack leader, but the established dog will be dominant to the puppy – and the puppy will accept this. He is used to his mother being the boss dog and to taking his place in the litter with his siblings, so he will expect the older dog to boss him about, and so must you.

Warning Growl

If, or more likely when, the old dog disciplines the puppy by turning him out of his bed, taking away a toy, giving a warning growl when he is eating, or giving a quick snap when he wants to be left alone to sleep, you must not interfere and take the puppy's part. Leave them to sort it out, and, unless you are very unlucky, they will soon settle into a satisfactory relationship.

A pup and an older dog should be introduced in the garden, where there is more space and fewer territorial issues.

CAR TRAVEL

Most dog owners like to take their dogs out with them, and the sooner you start taking your pup in the car, the more likely he is to enjoy travelling.

Car Sickness

Many pups are good travellers from the start, but some do suffer from car-sickness. If your puppy is prone to car-sickness, do not make the mistake of leaving him at home until he gets bigger. The chances are that he will be worse when he is older.

Sedatives or anti-sickness pills can often help; ask your vet to prescribe something suitable for your puppy's age and size. However, do not rely on using pills for every outing. Ginger is helpful in a lot of cases of travel sickness, in both humans and

In time, your pup will enjoy outings in the car.

dogs. The best solution is to accustom your puppy to the car, and, over a period of time, he should become a good traveller.

HEAT IS A KILLER

Cars can quickly turn into ovens, and many dogs have been literally cooked alive in cars. Even on a cool day, the oxygen inside a car quickly gets used up. It is absolutely essential to have adequate ventilation in any static car with a dog inside. But you should never leave your dog alone in a car in hot or warm weather.

CHOOSING A SAFE PLACE

You must decide where you want your puppy to travel in the car, bearing in mind that many dogs travel better when they cannot see out of the window.

The pup can travel in a crate or a dog box if you wish. Or you can fix a screw-eye on the floor of an estate car or station wagon and hook the pup on to it with a short lead with a swivel.

Before you start on a journey, make sure the pup has not been fed, and give him a chance to relieve himself. Put him on a collar and lead, and take along a friend (one who likes puppies, even messy ones) as a 'minder'. Make sure you are equipped with an old towel and some newspapers, just in case. If the pup is sick, do not make a fuss; clean him up, and, as soon as you can, stop the car and let him out for a short run. This is often enough to settle a pup and he will be all right afterwards.

Frequent Stops

Start with short trips and frequent stops. Try to go somewhere the puppy can safely run free, such as the local park. Let him out for a short run and then go on a little further and let him out again, perhaps on the way to a puppy class. Make the journeys fun; the puppy will not learn to enjoy the car if all he ever does is go to the shops or to the vet.

A crate is a safe, secure method of travel.

House rules should be established as soon as you bring the puppy home, so he grows up knowing what is – and isn't – acceptable behaviour.

SETTING THE HOUSE RULES

Start as you mean to go on. A friend of ours who trains dogs has a saying – 'Never sometimes'. As she says, it is a nonsensical phrase, but one that is well worth remembering.

An example of 'never sometimes' is if, when you are watching television, the pup creeps up beside you on the sofa. You think: "Well, he is rather cute", and let him stay. However, tomorrow Aunt Jane comes to visit, and she is not keen on dogs at the best of times. So, when your puppy enthusiastically jumps on her lap, you shout at him, pull him off the sofa and shut him in the kitchen.

In reality, it was your fault, not the pup's. So, you must play fair and decide what your puppy can and cannot do.

If he tries to come up on the sofa and you have decided that this is unacceptable, tell him "No", and send him to his own bed. Once he knows that is where he is meant to be, it will be easier for all of you.

Try to stick to the rules, which is often easier said than done if you have children in the family. But it is well worth the effort when you are rewarded with a well-behaved dog who knows what is expected of him without being told.

FIRST WORDS YOUR PUP MUST LEARN

Once the puppy has learned his name, which he should always associate with pleasure, he must next learn "No" and "Okay". "No" means "stop what you are doing now"; and "Okay" means just that. Do not shout at your puppy; he hears much better than you do. Growl out your "No", and praise him in a happy voice.

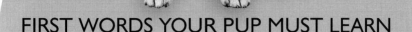

THE PUSHY PUPPY

Neither dogs nor puppies should go through doors or gates before you or any other member of the family. The behaviourists emphasise that this is to show your dominance over the pup, but it also has a practical purpose.

Puppies rushing through open doors can knock toddlers down, cause old people to fall, and trip up anyone in their way.

A pup who rushes out of the door could run into the road and get knocked down by a car, so this is a useful rule for everyone's benefit.

When the situation first arises, simply say "No" and use your hand to hold the puppy back. Once you are through the door, tell him "Okay" and pat him when he comes to you.

3 CARING FOR YOUR PUPPY

The dog is a carnivore, but a long association with man means that his tastes are now omnivorous.

Puppies have different needs from adult dogs. Young pups need three or four times the energy intake of an adult of the same breed. Not only do they need a basic maintenance allowance, but their energy intake must provide for activity and growth.

Like human babies, puppies have small stomachs, and, therefore, they need several small meals a day. At eight weeks, four meals a day

are sufficient, decreasing to one or two when adult. Small and Toy breeds mature early, usually at around six to nine months, but large and giant breeds may not reach adult weight until 18 or even 24 months.

IT DOESN'T ADD UP...

Do not be tempted by enticing adverts for minerals, vitamins and other supplements – all guaranteed to make your puppy into everything you want him to be. If you are feeding a balanced diet, that is sufficient. Extra minerals can do more harm than good, particularly if you are feeding a 'complete' diet.

CHOOSING A DIET

It is advisable to keep to the diet the pup is used to for the first few days. If you want to change the diet, do so gradually. There is a huge variety of puppy food on the market, and those made by reputable firms are mostly very good. You can take your pick from canned meat and/or dry food in a number of forms. What really matters is that the pup is fed a balanced diet, enjoys his food and thrives on it.

Manners

Although a pup should be left in peace to eat his food, he must be taught to accept the fact that you, or any of the family, have the right to go up to him when he is eating, or remove his food if you wish.

Start off by telling your puppy to "Sit" when you put down his food bowl, and then tell him he can eat. While he is eating, stroke him gently and talk to him. Most pups will be so busy eating, they will not even notice. But if your puppy growls at you, immediately growl back, grasp him by the scruff of his neck, and make him sit. Once he has calmed down, let him start eating again and stroke him. If your puppy is behaving well, drop a treat into his bowl to show him that you did not really want his dinner.

Teach the puppy to sit before he is given a meal.

33

WATCH THE WATER

A dog can go without food for several days, losing 40 per cent of his body weight without dying. However, with a water loss of 10-15 per cent, death can occur. Your puppy must have access to clean water all the time, especially if he is fed a dry diet. The exception to this is at night. You cannot expect a small pup to be dry at night if he has a large drink at 2am.

GETTING MEALTIMES RIGHT

Wild dogs and wolves eat only when they manage to catch their dinner, and their puppies, once weaned, can have a meal only when a member of the pack brings it back – and that certainly is not four times a day! Most wildlife parks feed their canines three or four times a week, as they remain much healthier that way. So, do not feel that you must stick to exact feeding times, or worry if your pup has to miss a meal for some reason or another. It will do the puppy no harm to wait a bit longer or have a meal a little earlier, if you find it necessary.

There is another advantage to varying feeding times. Puppies

Do not get stuck into too rigid a routine when feeding your puppy.

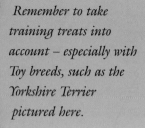

Remember to take training treats into account – especially with Toy breeds, such as the Yorkshire Terrier pictured here.

who are always fed 'on the dot' can develop into perfect pests when they grow up, demanding their dinner, come what may. Nothing is more aggravating than a dog who starts pestering and whining for his food at 11.45am when his feeding time is noon.

Not Too Late

So, start as you mean to go on and feed when you want to, not when the puppy asks for it. Do not give the last meal too late at night. We feed this meal at about 8pm, which gives the pup time to digest his meal before bedtime, and also encourages him to be clean through the night.

Never feed your puppy before taking him out in the car nor before vigorous exercise. If you have a Toy breed and you are training with treats, remember that a handful of tidbits is as much as a whole meal to a tiny pup. Try to achieve a balance, so you are not over-feeding.

DEALING WITH A PROBLEM FEEDER

Healthy puppies should be greedy puppies. If a healthy puppy says he does not want his dinner but begs you for something to eat, he is probably trying you out. Maybe he has smelled the chicken or salmon you were having for supper and fancies a bit. Do not give in to him.

If your puppy leaves his food, just take the bowl away and offer him fresh food at the next mealtime. No healthy puppy has ever starved himself to death, and, when your puppy realises that you are not going to offer him a series of different dishes to tempt his appetite, he will give in with good grace.

However, if your pup refuses his food and appears to be off-colour, this is a cause for concern and you should consult your vet.

GOLDEN RULES ON EXERCISE

All puppies – and dogs of whatever age, size or breed – need exercise. They also need to play, and, very often, the two can be happily combined. Young puppies should never be over-exercised, which means they should not be dragged on a lead for long walks or given too much free-running exercise. This particularly applies to the giant breeds, which mature more slowly.

Young pups need exercise and play, which will help them to develop both physically and mentally. If you are taking your pup to 'puppy classes', he will get quite a lot of exercise and will learn social canine manners by playing with the other puppies.

If you have a large garden or yard, you can play games with your puppy there, or you can take him to the local park and other open spaces where dogs are allowed.

Sensible exercise, which means never letting your puppy become really tired, can only do good. Never force a puppy to go on if he is getting tired, and do not make him jump over awkward or high obstacles until he is at least six, or even nine, months old.

Care should be taken not to over-exercise young pups – especially those of large breeds.

THE IMPORTANCE OF GROOMING

All dogs, from an Irish Wolfhound to a Chihuahua, need grooming, and it is also an important part of canine life. Wild dogs groom each other in an act of friendship, and this helps to cement the whole pack together.

In a domestic situation, the grooming session should always be something for the pup to enjoy; it should never become a battlefield. If it is properly carried

*Grooming strengthens canine bonds
and reaffirms friendships.*

out, grooming strengthens the bond between puppy and owner.

Few puppies need much grooming, and, if you have a short-coated breed, such as a Whippet, you may feel it is not worth bothering. This is definitely not the case. All puppies need to be handled, and you cannot start too soon. It will be time well spent, and a vet or a judge will appreciate a dog who behaves sensibly and allows himself to be handled without any fuss.

Grooming Acceptance

Once the puppy accepts being handled, place him on a table and start brushing.

The pup can be sitting, standing, or lying down. If you have a long-coated breed, grooming is easier if the dog learns to lie flat.

If the pup already knows how to lie down, give him a command, such as "Flat", and gently roll him on his side, keeping him there for a few

HANDLE WITH CARE!

Most puppies love being talked to and petted. When you have a spare moment, pick the pup up and sit with him on your lap. If you have a large puppy, just sit on the floor with him. Quietly coax the pup to sit still while you run your hands over him, open his mouth, pick up his feet, look in his ears, and rub his tummy. The object of the exercise is for the puppy to enjoy the experience. If your puppy wriggles, keep a firm hold on him until he relaxes, then praise him or give him a treat and finish for the day.

seconds. Once the puppy is relaxed, praise him and let him get up again.

Most breeds need only a few minutes of grooming daily, and a thorough grooming once a week.

That is, unless you have an Old English Sheepdog, an Afghan Hound, or a Pekingese. If this is the case, we hope you like grooming, as you will have to spend a lot of time doing it!

A toy will help the pup to view grooming as a positive experience.

A rubber brush or hound glove is ideal for short-coated breeds, such as this Bulldog puppy.

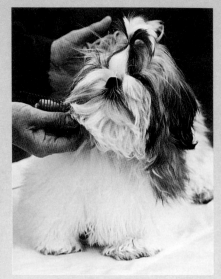

Long-coated breeds, such as this Shih Tzu, require a metal comb to remove tangles.

Smooth-Coated

If you have a smooth-coated breed, a hound glove is very useful. These usually have short rubber teeth on one side, and corduroy or velvet on the other. The rubber side is excellent for removing dead hairs, and the other side is for massaging and 'polishing'.

Long-Coated

A long-coated dog is more likely to develop mats and tangles in his coat. Gently comb out the hair using a steel comb, and check behind the ears and under the armpits, where mats are very likely to form. Knots or tangles should gently be teased out. Brush a small amount of coat at a time, making sure the bristles go right down to the skin, and work over the whole animal.

Wire-Haired

Wire-haired dogs, like Wire Fox Terriers, have harsh outer coats

THE PERFECT FINISH, WHATEVER HIS BREED

Terrier breeds, like this Jack Russell, need regular stripping to keep the coat tidy.

Thick-coated breeds, such as the Chow Chow pictured above, need a rake to remove shedding hair.

and dense, soft undercoats, which will need regular 'stripping'. This is usually done with a 'stripping knife', which looks rather like a penknife with serrated edges. All the terrier breeds are trimmed in different styles, and so, if you aim to show your puppy, you will need to seek professional help.

If you just want to keep your pup as a companion, you could learn to trim him yourself. Ask the breeder for advice or buy a book on the breed. In between

trims, this type of coat should only need regular brushing,

Stiff/Stand-Off

Breeds with stiff, stand-off coats, such as some of the Spitz breeds, should first have their coats brushed against the growth of the hair and then carefully brushed back into place. When these breeds have shed their coats, the amount of hair that comes out is unbelievable! A special rake can help to remove this more easily.

The Poodle does not moult but needs regular attention to prevent mats.

Non-Shedding

Poodles, and a few other breeds, do not shed their coats – which is a great help to any dog lover who suffers from asthma. This type of coat keeps on growing, and, unless it is properly looked after, it can end up in a matted mess.

Most Poodle owners use the services of a grooming parlour, although you can learn to do it yourself.

KEEPING NAILS IN CHECK

In the wild, canines wear their nails down naturally, but most dogs kept as companions will need to have their nails cut and/or filed regularly.

Some pups are very sensitive about their feet, so start handling the paws early on. Make a game of it, rolling the pup over, catching hold of his feet and playing with him. When the puppy accepts this, you can progress until the pup will lie still and allow you to examine his feet. Do not forget to reward the puppy when he does what you want.

When a dog is standing naturally, his nails should just touch the ground. If the nails are too long, it makes walking very uncomfortable.

To begin with, your puppy's nails may not need much attention, but it is good practice to keep the tips snipped off. Once the nails are allowed to grow too

To begin with, trim just the tips of the nails.

long, it is a difficult job to get them right again.

Buy some strong, good-quality nail-clippers. There are many different types to choose from, so just pick the type you prefer. A coarse file can be used to smooth off rough edges.

Avoiding The Quick

Light-coloured nails are much easier to clip than dark ones, because the quick, showing as a thin, pink line down the middle of the nail, is easily seen. Be very careful not to cut the quick; it is extremely painful, it bleeds profusely, and it can put a puppy off having his nails cut.

If your puppy has both light and dark nails, cut the light ones first. This will give you a better idea of how much to take off the dark nails, where you cannot see the quick.

If your puppy has dewclaws (usually located on the inside of the front legs), these must be checked regularly and trimmed if necessary.

Keep a close eye on dew claws, trimming when necessary.

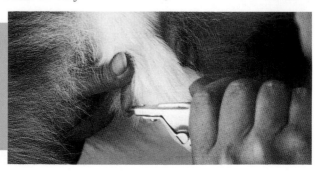

YOUR PUPPY'S TEETH

When you first have your puppy, he should have a set of 28 'baby' teeth, which, as you will soon discover, are unpleasantly sharp! Between four and seven months, the permanent teeth (averaging 42 in number) will start coming through, first the incisors and lastly the molars.

Unlike human babies, puppies rarely have teething troubles, but teething can cause a certain amount of stress, and puppies often become more sensitive to their environment during the teething period.

Most vets advise cleaning a dog's teeth about once a week. There are various 'doggy' toothpastes and toothbrushes on sale. With practice, your pup will soon learn to accept the attention.

Regular brushing will keep the teeth clean and the gums healthy.

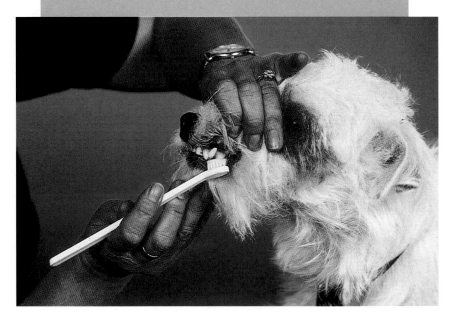

NATURAL CLEANING

Most dogs, like most people, develop tartar on their teeth – although this is unlikely to happen with a puppy or a young dog. If you keep the teeth in good condition while the dog is still young, it can help to prevent tartar forming. There are several things you can do to help. Make sure the pup has something hard to chew on, even if he has finished teething. Hard nylon toys, good-quality rubber toys, hard biscuits and marrow bones are all suitable.

TAKING AN EARLY BATH!

Dogs do not need regular bathing – once or twice a year is sufficient – unless your dog has rolled in something special!

Do not wait until your dog is fully grown before attempting his first bath, or you may have a struggle. If a young pup becomes accustomed to his bath, he will not resent it too much!

If possible, use a shower cubicle, with a non-slip rubber mat. Toy dogs can be bathed in the sink.

Use a shampoo specifically for dogs. Make sure the water is luke-warm, and apply the shampoo, working it into a lather. Rinse thoroughly, removing all traces of the shampoo. Dry with a towel, and then stand back as your dog has a good shake!

HEALTH MATTERS

In the first 12 months of life, hopefully, your puppy will experience minimal health problems. However, there are a number of preventative health programmes that should be adopted, and you, as the owner, must keep a check on any other problems that may arise.

Weekly Checks

Once a week, you should give your puppy a thorough grooming and check-up.

- Start at the head, looking at the eyes, which should be bright and clear.
- Next check the nose, which should be clear and free from discharge. In very dry, hot weather or in severe cold weather, the nose can sometimes become sore or cracked. If this is the case, a smear of olive oil, petroleum jelly or cod-liver oil will help.

- Open the mouth and check the teeth and gums. Gums should be healthy and pink in colour, although some breeds have black or black-spotted gums.
- Check the ears. If the ear is foul-smelling or has an unpleasant discharge, seek veterinary advice. However, you can easily clean off any normal dirt or wax with damp cotton-wool.
- Work down to the feet,

checking the pads for any cuts or cracks, and looking to see if the nails need to be trimmed. Look between and under the pads: some long-haired breeds tend to get mats in between the toes. If these are not cut out, they can cause lameness and sore feet.

● If you have a male puppy, check the penis and sheath. In a puppy or young dog any slight discharge should be light and clear. If there is a smelly or discoloured discharge, you should consult your vet.

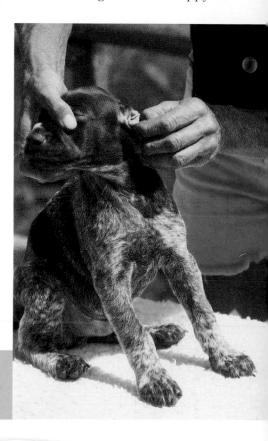

Weekly checks will alert you to any potential problems before they become unmanageable.

VACCINATIONS

Puppies are vaccinated against distemper, leptospirosis, hepatitis and parvovirus. In some countries where rabies is endemic, it is compulsory for dogs to be vaccinated against this disease. Depending on where you live, the timing of vaccinations will vary, so consult your vet.

INTERNAL PARASITES

Roundworms

Virtually all puppies have roundworms called *Toxocara canis*. Although pups can have worms without any tell-tale signs in their faeces, roundworms can often be seen as whitish-coloured thread-like objects, usually from 2-8ins (5-20cms) long. *Toxocara canis* can cause blindness in humans, but it very seldom does.

If your puppy is wormed on a routine basis, there will be no danger to you, your family or the general public.

Most vets recommend worming for roundworms in puppies at two, four, six, eight and twelve weeks. There are innumerable remedies available on the market. Many can be fed to the puppy with his normal meal. In fact, some wormers are now incorporated into the food.

Other Worms

There are other worms that affect dogs, tapeworms being the most common. Heartworms can affect dogs living in some parts of the United States.

The best course of action is to ask your vet to test your puppy, and recommend an appropriate preventative treatment.

You will need to plan a worming programme for your puppy.

EXTERNAL PARASITES

Fleas

The best-cared-for puppy can pick up fleas, especially if he comes into regular contact with other dogs. Grooming will help to keep your dog free from fleas, but you will also need to use some other preventative measure. There are a number of anti-parasitic flea sprays available, as well as spot-on treatments, which are effective.

Ticks

If you live in sheep- or deer-grazing areas, your puppy may pick up a tick. These parasites suck at the dog's blood until they become bloated. Do not be tempted to pull the tick from your puppy, as this will leave the mouth-piece implanted in the dog's skin. The best treatment is to apply some cotton-wool soaked in a mild antiseptic, and the tick will release its hold.

Tackle fleas with an anti-parasitic spray, or a spot-on treatment.

The most common problem a puppy is likely to suffer in the first 12 months of his life is diarrhoea. Withhold food for 24 hours, making sure that water is readily available, then give him something easy to digest, such as chicken or fish and rice. If the condition persists, ask your vet for advice. If you see signs of blood in the stools, contact your vet immediately.

49

4 UNDERSTANDING YOUR PUPPY

Dogs learn by association of ideas, as do all the higher animals. This simply means that, if an animal does something either accidentally or by persuasion and finds it pleasant, he will tend to do it again.

If it is unpleasant, he will be reluctant to do it again. We associate certain sights, sounds and smells with pleasant or unpleasant experiences.

A child can be told that touching the fire will be very painful, and, if he understands the spoken language, he is unlikely to try it out.

But the child who is not yet talking will not understand the danger, and may well put a finger in the fire – though he is very unlikely to do it again!

Correction and Reward

In order to get the dog to do what we want, and, just as important, to refrain from doing what we do not want, we build up desirable associations of ideas by a process of correction and reward. Correction could be described as any action that prevents the dog

Pushing the puppy into the sit position (left) is never as effective as rewarding the dog for sitting of his own accord (right).

from doing what he intends, or persuades him to do what the trainer wants him to do – such as pushing him into a sitting position.

Only the minimum of correction should ever be used, and, when the dog responds, no matter how reluctantly, he should be immediately rewarded. It is easy to over-correct, but it is very difficult to over-reward. To be effective it is essential that correction or reward is applied as the action takes place, or within seconds of it taking place. The vast majority of behavioural problems can be attributed to the

STRENGTH OF ASSOCIATION

As has already been pointed out, the strongest and most lasting associations are those created by fear. Following this are the first-time associations and those experiences that happen over and over again.

If a puppy is frightened by the first dog he meets, the effect will be far greater than if he had previously met friendly dogs. This is well known among dog show exhibitors. A puppy who has had a bad fright at his first show, for whatever reason, may be put off showing for life.

Bad Experience

But if he gets a fright after going to several shows, which he has enjoyed, the effect will be much less. And, of course, the effect will be greater if he has a bad experience at several shows in succession.

Another point to remember is that the effect of frightening experiences increases as the puppy gets older. A 16-week-old puppy may be absolutely terrified of something

that would not have affected him at all when he was seven weeks old.

A threatened animal can adopt one of three options: fight, flight, or freeze. Many dogs have been turned into fighters by being attacked when they were adolescents. However, it is rare for a young puppy to fight, no matter the provocation.

The pup will either freeze by

A bad experience can have a lasting effect on a dog's behaviour.

becoming submissive – probably rolling on his back and waving his paws in the air; or he will flee, which is the biggest danger of all. First, there is the very real danger that the puppy might run into the path of an oncoming car. But that is not the only danger.

Running Scared

The instant the puppy bolts, he has separated himself from his protector, and the further he runs, the greater does the separation become, with the puppy becoming even more terrified. So much so that, by the time the pursuer decides to give up the chase, the puppy is completely disorientated. One experience of this sort has left many a bold, friendly puppy terrified of strange dogs for life.

Like all experiences, this one can create different associations. The most likely is that the dog will be afraid of strange dogs, or he may only be afraid of the type of dog that frightened him.

We have a Chihuahua who was frightened by a black dog, and, years later, he is still afraid of black dogs – but he is not frightened of dogs of any other colour.

Additionally, the puppy may associate the fright with the place, and he may be afraid of going near the spot where the incident took place, even when there is no dog there.

RELATING TO OTHER DOGS

It goes against the laws of nature for an adult dog to attack a submissive puppy, and it is very rare to find one that does. But it is natural for any dog to chase anything that runs away, be it a child, a sheep, a puppy, or a ball rolled along the ground.

If a strange dog comes bounding up, put your puppy on a lead to make sure he does not flee. Do not drag the pup away from the other dog; do not scream at him "Come here!", and do not pick him up. In short, do not do anything that might give the impression that there is anything to be frightened of.

When they are afraid, some puppies will run to their owners for protection. Others stand their ground until the last minute, then lose their nerve and take off.

Frightened pups often run to their owners for protection.

If the strange dog proves to be friendly, allow him to sniff the puppy, but do not touch either of them, and do not offer the puppy treats while the interaction is taking place.

PUPPY CLASSES

Puppy classes, where your puppy can meet other youngsters in a controlled environment before going out into the big, wide world, can be a great help. In this situation, puppies also have the opportunity to mix with new people, both adults and children.

INSTINCT AND INTELLIGENCE

It is doubtful whether anything causes so much confusion in the minds of dog owners as the relationship between instinct and intelligence.

To the vast majority of owners, the outstanding feature of any dog, especially their own, is his intelligence. But, in fact, the reason why the dog has become such a valuable servant and friend to mankind is because of his instincts. Most dogs are sufficiently intelligent to be able to learn anything we want to teach them, provided the right instincts are there.

Both instinct and intelligence can be an asset or a liability. The submissive dog is likely to use his intelligence to understand the wishes of the owner. The dominant dog is just as likely to use his intelligence to find ways of evading his owner's wishes. We spent many years training, or re-training, so-called difficult and disobedient dogs belonging to other people. Virtually all of these dogs were very intelligent – often more so than their owners, which was usually the cause of the problem!

The importance of a dog's instincts should not be underestimated.

Terriers were bred to go to ground, and there are many pet terriers that can't resist following a scent down a hole.

INSTINCTIVE BEHAVIOUR

Instinct makes an animal do something without any learning. The first instinct is the instinct to survive, which makes the newborn puppy squirm around until he finds a teat and then start sucking. As he grows up, other instincts develop. These vary according to the breed, and they also vary in strength between individuals of the same breed. All breeds have inherited some hunting instinct from the wolf. By careful selective breeding, man has strengthened this instinct in some breeds until it is stronger than in its wild ancestor. The wolf only hunts when it is hungry, but many dog breeds will hunt just for the sake of hunting.

THE HERDING INSTINCT

The herding instinct in the modern Border Collie is an example of the extent to which man can develop an instinct for his own purpose. Contrary to common belief, it is not because of his superior intelligence that the Border Collie reigns supreme in sheepdog trials – it is because of the breed's instinct to herd.

The average Labrador Retriever is just as intelligent as the average Border Collie, but a Labrador will not work sheep because he has no herding instinct.

The herding instinct in the modern Border Collie is often over-developed to the extent that many of the breed are obsessed with working.

Good Example

This is a good example of how an instinct that can be an asset to one owner can be a liability to another. To anyone wanting to compete in sheepdog trials, the herding instinct in his dog cannot be too strong. But that sort of dog will herd anything from the neighbour's cat to a double-decker bus, which can obviously lead to trouble!

If a pup is not allowed to use an instinct, that instinct will usually become weaker and perhaps die out completely. A sheepdog puppy who is prevented from working when the instinct is developing may refuse to take any interest in sheep by the time he is a year old.

However, he may well become 'hooked' on something like horses, cars, or bikes. If you want a dog to work, start him when he wants to 'run'. If you do not want him to work, do not let him start – find something else into which he can channel his energy.

The herding instinct can be a liability in the pet dog.

THE RETRIEVING INSTINCT

Other breeds have instincts that have been developed by man for various purposes, and this includes the retrievers (which include several different breeds) and most spaniel breeds. Dogs of this breeding will usually pick up objects and carry them around without any training or encouragement, although the age at which they start showing this instinct can vary between individuals.

All dogs enjoy having something to do: a large number get into trouble because they are unemployed. One way to overcome this is to make use of the instincts that your type of dog has inherited. If you have a spaniel of a retriever pup, encourage him to bring your slippers or pick up the mail.

THE HUNTING INSTINCT

Hound puppies frequently have a stronger hunting instinct than the wild dog. They can be divided into two groups: sighthounds, who hunt by sight, and scenthounds, who hunt by using their noses.

Sighthounds include such breeds as Afghans, Salukis, Greyhounds and Whippets. There is organised racing in which most sighthounds can take part – you can usually get the particulars from the breed clubs. There is also organised racing specifically for Greyhounds and Whippets.

Scenthounds do not bother to look – they simply put their noses down and follow the track of their quarry. Beagles and Basset Hounds are well-known members of this group.

Greyhounds are driven by the instinct to chase.

THE GUARDING INSTINCT

The guarding instinct probably affects more dog owners than any other instinct. Most people like to think that their dog would protect them if the occasion arose, and in fact the majority of all breeds (including crossbreeds and mongrels) will attempt to do so. If you have a Rottweiler, German Shepherd Dog, Dobermann or other guarding breed, you might wish to go in for Working Trials, where the dog can partake in tracking and police work. Schutzhund training is very popular in the USA and Europe. Some breeds, such as those mentioned, have been bred specifically as guards and have a very strong guarding instinct, which needs experienced handling.

5 TRAINING EXERCISES

Different people want their pups to learn different things, but it is fairly safe to say that most people want a dog who is clean in the house, walks quietly on a lead, sits and lies down on command, and comes when called.

THE RECALL

Before tackling this exercise, let us first solve the problem of why so many dogs refuse to come when called. The answer is that their owners have taught them not to respond. This is almost certainly unintentional, but the result is the same.

It happens in many ways, such as calling the puppy, and then shouting when he does not come because he is investigating a

fascinating new scent. When the pup eventually decides that he has satisfied his curiosity, he returns to his owner, who promptly grabs hold of him and scolds him for not coming when called.

But as far as the pup is concerned, he has been told off for coming – as that was the last thing he did. Always call your pup in a happy, cheerful voice, and praise him well when he comes to you.

Name Drain

Do not keep on calling him for no reason; if you keep on shouting his name, he will soon treat it like any other background noise. As already mentioned, dogs understand sounds, not words, and they associate certain sounds with certain actions. One of the first, if not the first, association that any puppy should learn is that if he responds to his name, he will be rewarded.

Use food as a reward, but not every time.

Rewards Not Bribes

Food is very useful, especially for puppies, but your object is to have a dog who obeys whether you have food or not. Your pup should never demand food for doing a certain action. If he is only given food at odd intervals, then he will not come to regard it as a right.

You want your pup to learn that coming to you means a reward.

LEAD-TRAINING

Although you had your pup on a collar and lead to bring him home, he should learn to walk properly as soon as possible. Many pups do not bother at all when a collar is first put on, but others scratch and generally protest for quite a while. Just ignore all the drama; the pup will accept the collar in time.

Make sure you use a light, soft collar; it should not be too tight, nor so slack that the pup can get it off or get his jaw caught in it. Always take the collar off at night.

You should not start lead-training until your puppy will follow you without being on a lead. The lead is not something to make a dog go with the owner; it is a safety line to prevent him running away, and a means of controlling him when he is learning new exercises.

Be Positive

If your pup struggles when you first put on the lead, do not fight with him or drag him after you. Stand still, and, as soon as the puppy relaxes, make a great fuss of him and encourage him with food to come up to you. Walk on a

The collar should be light and soft.

little way, holding a treat in your hand, which should encourage the puppy to follow you. Do not go more than a few paces before giving a reward. Some pups are motivated by toys, and you can encourage a reluctant puppy to follow you by showing him a toy, and then rewarding him with a game when he has followed you for a few paces.

A toy or treat will encourage the puppy to walk on lead.

THE PULLING PUP

Most pups are soon trotting along quite happily, some so happily that they start pulling – a habit that needs stopping straight away. If the pup pulls, give him a sharp jerk, not a hefty one to throw him head over heels. Once he has stopped, call him back to you, praise him well and start off again. You could also try standing still as soon as the puppy starts pulling. It takes two to pull, and the pup will not get any fun out of it if you will not 'play'. Once the puppy is behaving, tell him he is a good boy and start walking again, talking to him and trying to keep his attention.

TEACHING THE SIT AND DOWN

Teach the 'Sit' before the 'Down'. Call your puppy to you, and, when you have his attention, hold your hand just above his head, at the same time saying "Sit".

As your pup looks up at the treat, he will sit.

As the pup looks up, move your hand towards the back of his head, and, as his eyes follow your hand movements, he should automatically sit.

As soon as he sits, give him a treat and praise him well, but not too enthusiastically as this will make him excited and he may get up. If the puppy shows signs of moving, place your hand on his rump to keep him there for a few seconds. Then tell him "Okay" and let him get up. Repeat this four or five times, but do not keep on or he will only get fed up. When you have finished the lesson, have a game together.

The Down

Once your puppy knows how to sit on command, you can start teaching him the 'Down'. First, command your puppy to sit and

Use a treat to lure your pup into the Down position.

attract his attention. Hold your hand, with a treat in it, in front of the pup's head, say "Down" and lower your hand to the ground just in front of him. As he goes down, praise him and give him the treat.

Place your other hand on the puppy's shoulders to keep him there a moment before letting him up. If he is reluctant about going down, use your other hand from the start to press down on his shoulders.

PLAY TRAINING

Once your puppy has mastered the basic exercises, you may wish to teach him some play exercises. This will be fun for you and your family, and it will result in a happier dog who receives plenty of stimulation and is eager to respond to his owner.

Shaking Hands

Perhaps the simplest trick of all is

shaking hands. In fact, some dogs do it without ever being taught. If your pup is the sort who offers up a paw, take it and reward him with a treat, giving him a command at the same time. Soon he should realise that this action pleases you, and he should do it every time you ask him.

If your puppy is not a 'natural', you may have to start by giving a command and tapping his leg until he lifts it. When he responds, make a great fuss of him and reward him.

If your pup offers a paw, reward him and give a command.

TEACHING YOUR PUPPY TO BEG

This should not be taught too soon. It puts a strain on the back of an immature pup, especially a long-legged breed. However, as with shaking hands, some pups teach themselves to beg. Small, stocky pups are less likely to damage themselves, but you must still be careful. With a small dog, all that is usually needed is to have him sit, tell him to beg, hold a treat just above his head, and encourage him to sit up. If this does not work, treat him as you would a larger breed. Take your puppy to a corner, which will support his back as he sits up. Tell him to sit, hold his front paws in one hand and tell him to beg, holding a treat over his head with the other hand. Then gently lift his front paws up until he is in the right position. Make sure he is properly balanced. Once the puppy starts to go up on his own, be ready to support him if he loses his balance. Like many tricks, some dogs learn this quickly, but others will need a lot of your patience.

It is usually easier to teach small breeds to beg.

When your pup has mastered catching treats, you can try a toy.

THE ART OF CATCHING

We have always taught our dogs to catch food thrown to them, which makes it easy to get them to 'stand to attention' in front of a judge. It also makes it easy to reward a dog immediately he does what is wanted. A lot of dogs are natural catchers, others fail to see the point at all. It is best to start with food.

Call the pup to you, stand a little way back, tell him to catch, making sure he is watching your hand, and throw or half-drop the treat towards his mouth.

If your puppy misses, pick up the treat, do not let him have it, and try again. If he manages to catch it, stop, and start again the next day. As your puppy improves, gradually stand further back until he will catch it from quite a distance. Once he is catching well, he can be taught to catch a ball – make sure it is large enough so that he cannot swallow it – and, later on, you can play Frisbee with him.

If your puppy shows an aptitude for catching, you may like to try him at Flyball when he is fully grown.

SPEAK ON COMMAND

This is not really a trick, as it has many practical uses, such as warning you when visitors arrive. Watch your pup and find out what makes him bark. It may be when he is going for a walk, when you start playing with him, when the doorbell rings, or when he wants his dinner. When your puppy does bark, tell him "Speak" and reward him. Put a lot of enthusiasm into it, as you want him to be excited. Even if it takes a while, this is well worth teaching. In fact, the easiest way to stop a noisy dog from barking is to teach him to bark on command – and then to teach him to stop barking!

PLAYING HIDE-AND-SEEK

Start off by playing hide-and-seek with children doing the hiding, and you can then progress to hiding a toy or some other object. Start by throwing the object out a short distance where the puppy can see it, and send him to fetch it. Increase the distance and throw the object into long grass where the pup has to look for it.

RETRIEVING

There are several methods of teaching the retrieve, but we will concentrate on the play method. This is really just a question of encouraging the retrieving instinct, rather than teaching a specific action, as we do when teaching the 'Down'.

Here the operative word is 'play'. Children can often encourage a puppy to retrieve far quicker than their parents. They are less inhibited and do not feel they are 'making fools of themselves' by talking baby language, or even getting on all fours to encourage the puppy to play.

The object you use to teach the retrieve does not really matter, as long as you choose something that the puppy likes and that is easy to carry. Never try to force him to pick up something that he obviously dislikes. Use something that is easy for both of you to hold, such as a stuffed sock or soft toy.

Odd though it sounds, it is much easier to teach a puppy to let go of something he likes than to teach him to hold on to something that he has decided he would rather spit out! If the puppy refuses to release the object, a treat offered on a fair exchange basis will usually persuade him to let go.

The retrieve can be encouraged through play.

69

6 GROWING UP

In the human race, adolescence is widely recognised as a problematic time for youngsters, a time when the body undergoes major physical changes, and, as maturity approaches, parental authority is challenged.

Some teenagers are more prone to get into serious trouble at this stage, and this is often attributed to lack of discipline in childhood, and lack of useful employment and stimulation. Very much the same applies to dogs.

It is normal for puppies to be disciplined by their mother for as long as they are with her.

If this discipline is continued by the new owner, the pups are less likely to cause trouble when they become 'teenagers' than those who have been allowed to run wild. In the early stages, most of the training can be applied by reward, whereas later on some correction will almost certainly be necessary.

WHEN YOUR PUP REACHES ADOLESCENCE

The age at which a puppy becomes adolescent varies between breeds and individuals of the same breed. Generally speaking, small breeds mature much more quickly than large ones.

Yorkshire Terriers are quite often as mature at six months as some Irish Wolfhounds are at two years. The level of testosterone, especially in the male, is at its peak at about this time. Quite suddenly, this can make the pup feel 'grown up', and that there is much more to life than obeying his owner. The opposite sex becomes more interesting and the marking of territory more important. Signs of dominance may appear for the first time, and sometimes the first signs

Small dogs and Toy breeds tend to mature at an earlier age.

of aggression, especially towards other dogs.

This subject is rarely discussed, with the result that owners are taken by surprise and think that something has 'gone wrong', when it is a perfectly normal process of growing up. If you realise this, and treat your dog as a young adult rather than a puppy, you should not have a great problem.

A large breed such as the Irish Wolfhound will not mature until two years of age.

THE IN-SEASON BITCH

The first indication of adolescence in the bitch is when she comes in season. The age at which this happens varies considerably, some coming in season as early as six months and others not until twelve months or older.

This is a very traumatic experience for the bitch. Not only does she have to cope with hormonal changes, which affect her both mentally and physically, it is also inevitable that her lifestyle will change to some degree.

Behaviour will change during the bitch's first season.

Isolation

For a start, she will have to be kept away from male dogs. Quite apart from the sexual attraction of the moment, some of these dogs may have been her friends and playmates since puppyhood. Suddenly, and for no reason that she can understand, she is not allowed to see them at all. Not surprisingly, the behaviour of some bitches changes dramatically at this stage, and occasionally the change is permanent. It is important to prevent the bitch from feeling that she is no longer wanted.

No attempt should be made to teach new exercises, especially any lessons that she does not like very much. Play games with her, and indulge her in anything she enjoys doing.

THE CASE FOR NEUTERING

Neutering remains a controversial subject, with potential for an endless source of debate.

Unless we want to use an individual for breeding, all our dogs are castrated and our bitches are spayed. We have found that any change in behaviour – and there is very little change – is for the better as far as the owner is concerned. Spaying also removes the risk of pyometra, an illness common among older breeding bitches.

There is some difference of opinion as to the best age to operate. Many vets recommend castration before the puppy is four months old, arguing that it is a simpler operation at that age. But vets do not live with their patients and rarely know what changes have taken place.

Our own observations suggest that dogs castrated too soon fail to mature mentally. They lack initiative and they are liable to obesity, which does not happen if castration is left until the dog matures. The best guide to this is when the dog starts lifting his leg.

Our own bitches are not spayed until after their first season. However, we have known of bitches spayed at around six or seven months when they had not come in season, with no ill effects.

Neutering should be discussed with your vet.

73

UNDERSTANDING DOMINANCE

In a dog pack there are varying degrees of dominance, but there is always one dominant leader. Fortunately for us, the dog is quite happy to allow the human animal to take on the role of the leader, and there is no shortage of advice as to how this should be done. Nevertheless, some important points are often overlooked.

Born Leaders

Some dogs are born to be leaders, but, as with humans, the majority are quite happy to be led. The idea that every puppy must be dominated from the word go leads to many submissive puppies failing to develop initiative. Far from being dominated, such puppies must be brought out of themselves if they are to develop into confident adults.

Dominance is relative. A dog that is dominant towards one person may be submissive towards another. Many dogs are dominant towards one member of the family and submissive towards

We are fortunate that the dog is happy to accept his owner in the role of leader.

another. The person who finds it difficult to control their own small children will inevitably fail with a dominant dog. However, they may form a perfectly good relationship with a more submissive type who has no desire to challenge their authority.

We believe that dominance has come to the fore partly as a result of the modern cult of the 'kind' trainer. We are certainly not advocating unkind or even harsh training: respect, not fear, should be the aim. In any case, cruelty or unkindness are terms that cannot readily be defined – they mean different things to different people.

Different Responses

What is cruel to one dog is not at all cruel to another. For instance, to jerk a Whippet or a Greyhound on a chain slip collar would be extremely cruel, but a Bull Terrier would not even feel it. Different breeds have different responses, and within each breed there is a whole range of temperaments. The successful dog owner assesses a dog on the basis of observation,

Some dogs are naturally more dominant, but training can ensure that the dog does not become too assertive.

rather than trying to apply dog training theories, regardless of the dog's individual character.

A dominant dog does not necessarily represent a failure on the part of the owner; over the years, we have had many dominant dogs, including some of our very best workers. If the pup with a dominant nature is correctly reared and trained (as outlined in earlier chapters), a relationship of mutual respect is established and there is no reason why any problems should arise.

A BALANCED RELATIONSHIP

The aim of every dog owner is to achieve a happy, balanced relationship with their dog. The dog should respect the 'pack leader' and be secure in the knowledge that he is a valued member of the pack – but not the most important member.

COPING WITH BAD BEHAVIOUR

Just like teenagers, your adolescent dog will have good days and bad days. You will just have to learn to live with this for a while, and make the most of the good days. Sometimes, your dog will behave like an overgrown puppy, and another day he will think he is a 'big macho dog' who has no intention of obeying you at all.

In this situation, do not fight with him – it will only make matters worse. Above all, never give a command that is likely to be ignored and that you cannot enforce. The best remedy is to play with your dog – games such as chasing a ball or playing hide-and-seek with a favourite toy – and generally providing plenty of exercise.

There will be good days and bad days, but you will win through in the end!

Although your dog may not realise it, he is still getting some training, although he is enjoying himself and sees it all as fun. However, if the dog persists in doing things that you really cannot allow, put him on a lead, command him to go in the Down, and make sure he stays in that position for a reasonably long period. No exercise has a more sobering effect on a dog.

Short and Cheerful

Remember that young dogs have a very short attention span. So do not start giving long training sessions; your dog will only become bored and will be easily distracted.

Keep training sessions short and cheerful, always ending on a good, positive note. You will achieve far more than if you keep nagging at your dog in long, tedious training sessions.

You also run a very real risk of your dog learning to dread training sessions – and then all progress will be at a complete standstill.

Giving your dog fun tasks to do will keep him mentally stimulated.

AVOIDING TEMPTATION

The adolescent dog finds it almost impossible to resist temptation, so avoid situations where your dog is likely to disobey house rules. Do not give him the opportunity to steal the Sunday roast by leaving him alone in the kitchen. If you are going out without your dog, do not leave him in a room where he can tear up your best rug. When your cat is sitting sunning itself in the garden, do not let your dog out so he can chase it. The last thing you want at this stage is a showdown. Confrontation will start a battle of wills, and all the good work you have done in building a relationship with your dog will be ruined. The vast majority of young dogs wil soon settle down, and peace and harmony will be restored.

PRAISE AND STIMULATION

If you have spent time socialising and training your puppy through his early days, you will be repaid a hundredfold. Remember, we all work better when we are praised, so never forget to reward and praise your dog for doing the right thing, even after he has been trained and has performed the exercise correctly on innumerable occasions. After all, why should your dog try to please you if he gets nothing in return?

Like humans, a dog never stops learning. The more you teach your dog, the more he will learn and the happier he will be. Make sure he has something to do – fetching your slippers, collecting the mail, or barking to alert you when the doorbell rings.

When you go for a walk, vary the route and give your dog something different to do, such as searching for a ball, swimming, or retrieving. These things will help to form a bond of friendship between you.

Take your dog to training classes; even if you do not end up with an Obedience champion, you can have a lot of fun, and your dog will benefit from the time you are working together.

Other Activities

As your dog reaches maturity, consider other activities, such as Agility, Working Trials, or Flyball.

We all know the saying "the devil finds work for idle hands". Substitute "paws" for "hands" and this is equally true of your dog. A bored dog is certain to get into trouble, whereas a well-trained, well-balanced dog will be a pleasure to you and your family for the duration of his life.

The devil makes work for idle paws – a canine sport will use up a lot of physical and mental energy, which could otherwise be spent mischief-making.

ABOUT THE AUTHORS

Professional dog trainers John and Mary Holmes spent a lifetime working with dogs, breeding them, caring for them, and training them. They have helped many handlers to solve problems with their dogs, as well as training their own dogs for a wide range of tasks – from film and television work to Obedience competitions and farm work.

They have bred and shown pedigree dogs under the Formakin kennel name, and they were responsible for importing the Australian Cattle Dog to Britain.

John, who died in 2000, was an international Championship show judge, and his appointments included judging at Crufts. A well-known contributor to the canine press, he wrote several books on training the family dog and the working dog. Mary has served on the committee of the Australian Cattle Dog Society.